# READY TO DA

Written by
Tara Rao

Illustrations by
Priya Krishnan Das

Dedication

I dedicate this book to my grandmother, Prabha (Amma) and my mom, Pratima for taking me taking me to all my dance and music classes and encouraging me to dance my heart out, always!

It was fall again and I was ready for the 5th grade at my elementary school in Brooklyn, New York.

It had been a whole year since I moved back to the United States after living in India for some time.

Lots of changes with moving to a new home, new school and new friends!

school
Speed
limit
20

When in India, I had to learn 3 languages, different foods, customs and culture. But I was determined to make the most of it. I lived with my grandparents in Chennai, India where art, music, dance is all around you!

My grandmother knew that I loved to sing and dance. I was always humming or singing songs or dancing my own dance in the kitchen while she cooked.

Dances of India
BHANGRA
KATHAK
LAVANI
MANIPURI
KATHAKALI
BHARATNATYAM

She enrolled me in vocal and dance lessons as soon as the school year started. I was hooked!

But it wasn't ballet, tap or jazz. It was Bharatnatyam and Carnatic music. I had never seen or heard this form of art and it was fun!

I enjoyed it so much that after returning to the United States, my Mom found me new teachers or gurus as they call them in India, for both dance and music.

My fifth grade teacher, Mr. Valentino, asked the class to write about our summer holidays and share it with the class.

I wrote about my busy summer in India, with my grandparents and lots of dancing and singing. He enthusiastically said, "you must dance or sing for the class!"

I was embarrassed at first but was excited to share what I loved to do outside of class. I was a little afraid of what the other students might think.

I was the only Indian student in my class and only one of a few in the whole school.

I had a little trouble with some of the students and got teased when I first came to the school.

But I took it as a challenge! I had never performed in front of an audience before. I ran home that day excited to tell my Mom and my dance teacher!

I practiced and practiced! As the day grew closer and closer to my class performance, I was growing nervous.

The day before my performance, Mr. Valentino really encouraged me and said that I will really be sharing something special with the whole class. I could not help but feel happy and excited!

The big day arrived! I was super excited to go to school that morning.

I got my boom box with the music my dance teacher gave me, and a simple outfit called the salwar kameez.

I wore my favorite salwar kameez, it was a yellow top with red mango leaves and red pants.

Traditionally, a Bharatnatyam dance dress is worn for all dance performances. It has many layers of fabric with designs.

The dancer wears jewelry for the head, earrings, necklaces, bangles for the wrists and a belt around the waist. And bells around the ankles so you can hear every step the dancer makes!

As I entered my classroom that morning in my yellow and red salwar kameez, I felt knots in my stomach! But my best friends had big grins on their faces and so did my teacher!

Mr. Valentino got up from his desk and said, "Attention Class!" "Before we start our lessons today, we have a special performance by one of our students, Tara Rao!"

I was very nervous and had knots in my tummy but try to smile as big as I could.

"How much room do you need Tara?" "Ummm, the front of the classroom would be enough." "You heard her class, clear the front!"

My fellow classmates swung into action to clear the front of the classroom of desks and chairs. Mr. Valentino enthusiastically said, "Ok Tara, we are ready to be dazzled!"

Okay,
Tara, we are ready to be dazzled!
Bharatnatyam
by
Tara Rao

As I made my way to the front of the class with my boom box, I felt the butterflies not just in my tummy but flying around me! I was excited but nervous at the same time.

I plugged my boom box in and proceeded to pray to Mother Earth, the Gods above and my audience in what was called the "Namaskar."

I asked my friend sitting next to the boom box to hit play.

The music started and so did I. I was so nervous that I hardly noticed everyone sitting just a few feet away.

I took a deep breath, smiled and went to my dance zone.

The steps poured out of me like it never had before!

Before I knew it, my three minute dance piece was over! After the music stopped, I did my end "Namaskar" and smiled as the whole class was clapping their hands together and my teacher and some friends whistled in excitement!

I was a little embarrassed but totally thrilled that everyone enjoyed it!!

clap clap
essay for the week.
clap clap
Winners
clap clap
clap clap

After I caught my breath and the class settled down, Mr. Valentino exclaimed, "What a performance and what talent! Let's give Tara another round of applause, class!"

The class clapped and whistled! I was so thrilled that I remembered all my steps and was able to share such a dance form with my class.

Mr. Valentino, then asked me if I wouldn't mind taking a few questions from my classmates. "Sure!" I said.

I got asked a whole lot of questions such as "why do you dance barefoot?" and "how do you move your head from side to side?"

Why do you dance barefoot?
How do you move your head from side to side?
essay for the week.
Winners

It was fun answering everyone's questions and sharing my passion for an ancient art form, Bharatnatyam.

I am so glad that my teacher encouraged me to share my talent and that I was able to perform in front of my class.

No one had experienced such culture, music and dance before! I went on to dance on many other stages and in front of different audiences all over the country and world!

The End.

Made in the USA
Monee, IL
19 January 2022